ModernGuitar Playalong

Published 2003
© International Music Publications Limited
Griffin House, 161 Hammersmith Road, London, W6 8BS, England
Editorial, new arrangements and engraving, and recording by Artemis Music Limited

GW00724800

Cochise

Words and Music by Christopher Cornell, Timothy Commerford, Tom Morello and Brad Wilkes

Don't Think You're The First

Words and Music by James Skelly

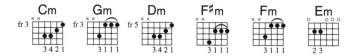

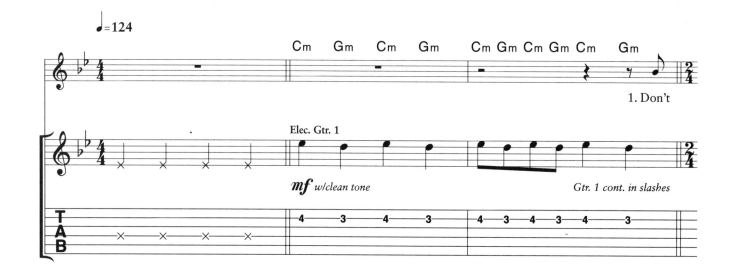

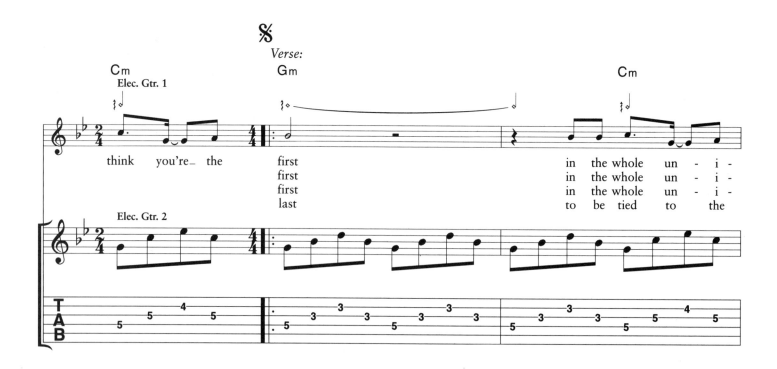

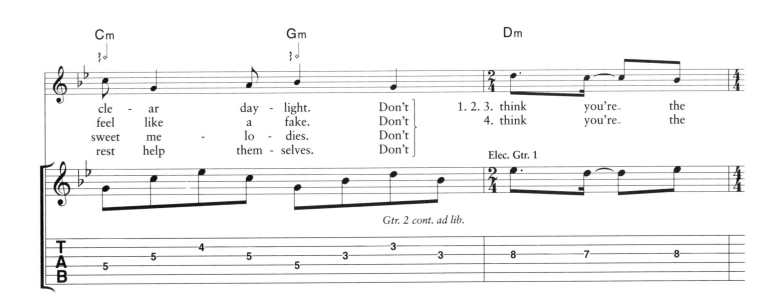

Chorus:

To Coda ⊕

Interlude:

4. Don't think you're the

Out Of Time

Words by Albarn
Music by Albarn, James and Rowntree

Pain Killer

Words and Music by Olly Knights and Gale Paridjanian

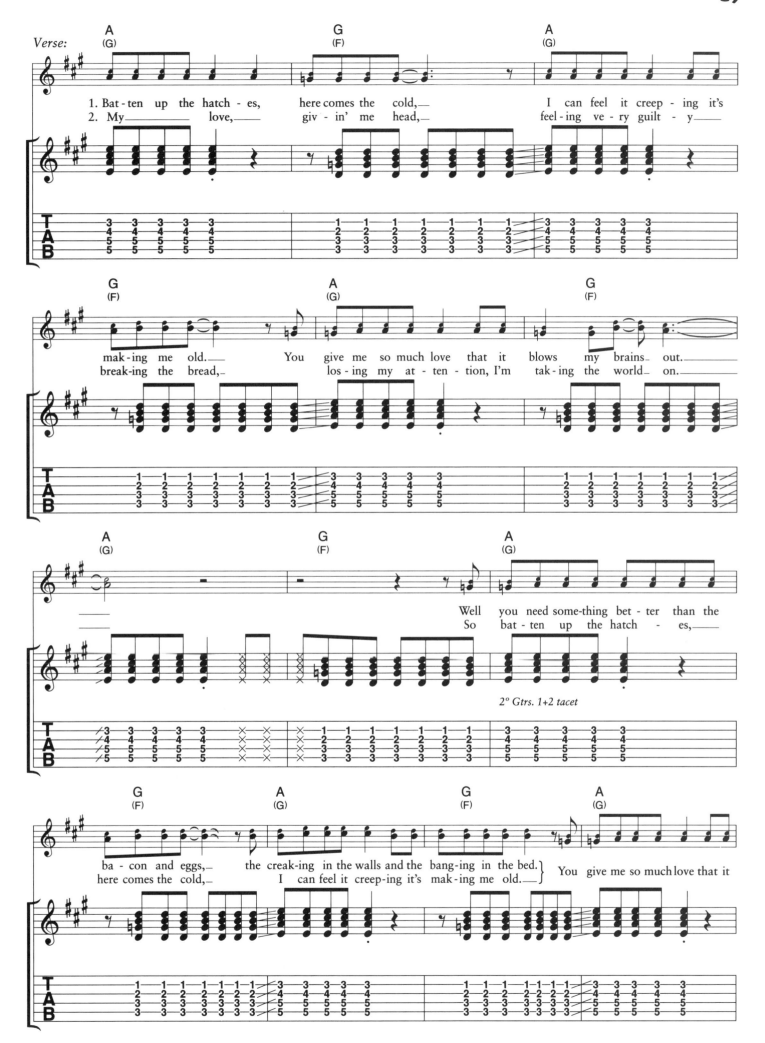

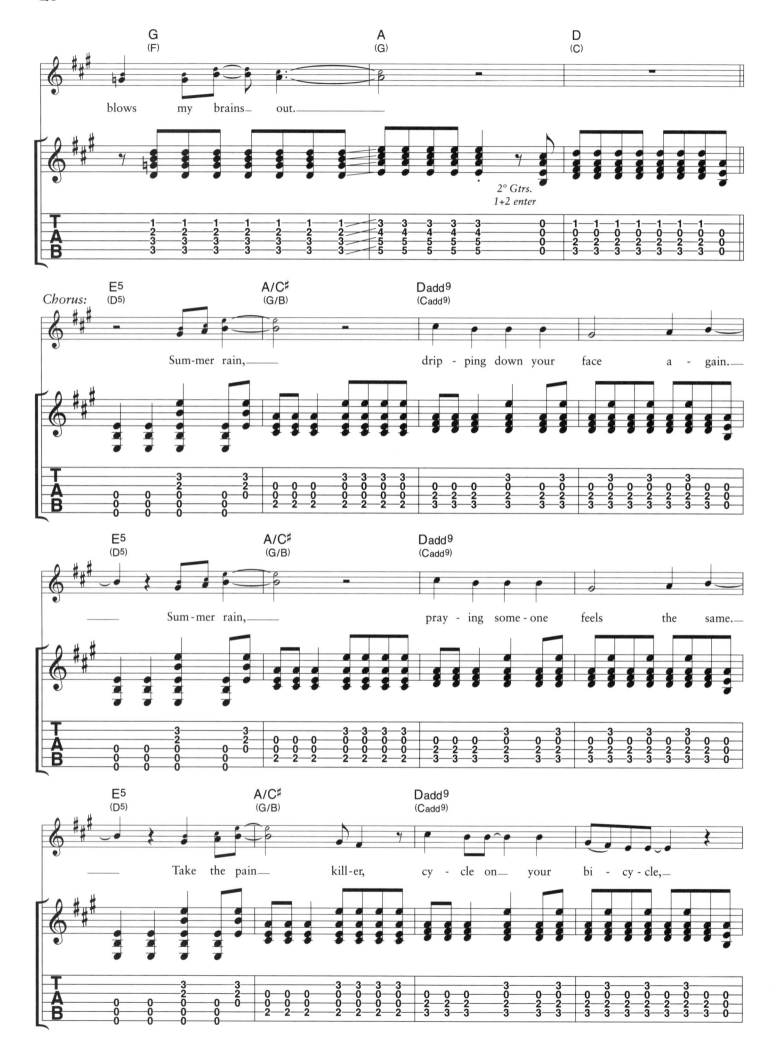

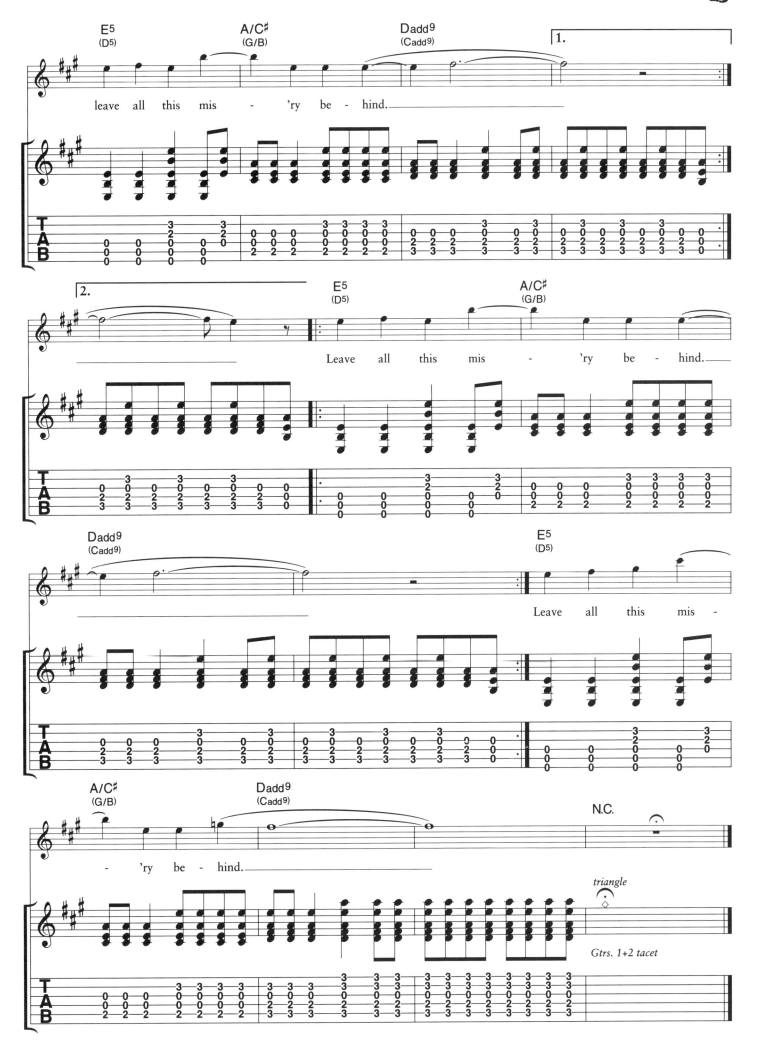

Pounding

Words and Music by Jimi Goodwin, Jez Williams and Andy Williams

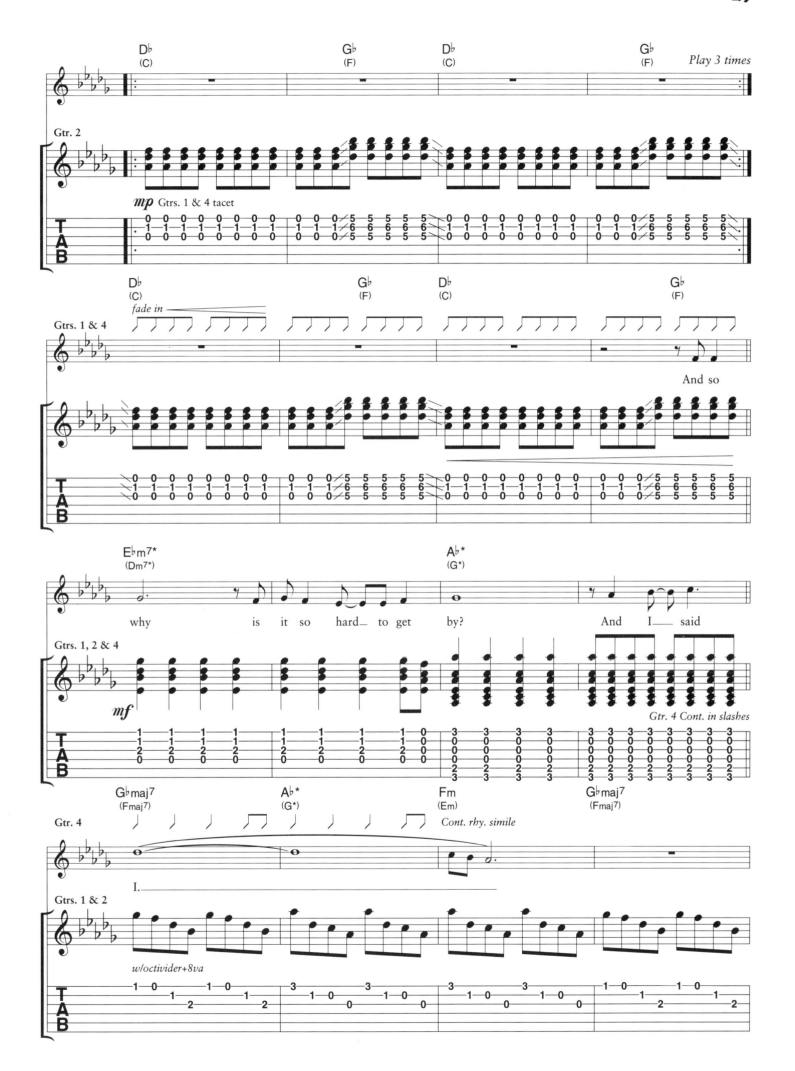

Seven Nation Army

Words and Music by Jack White

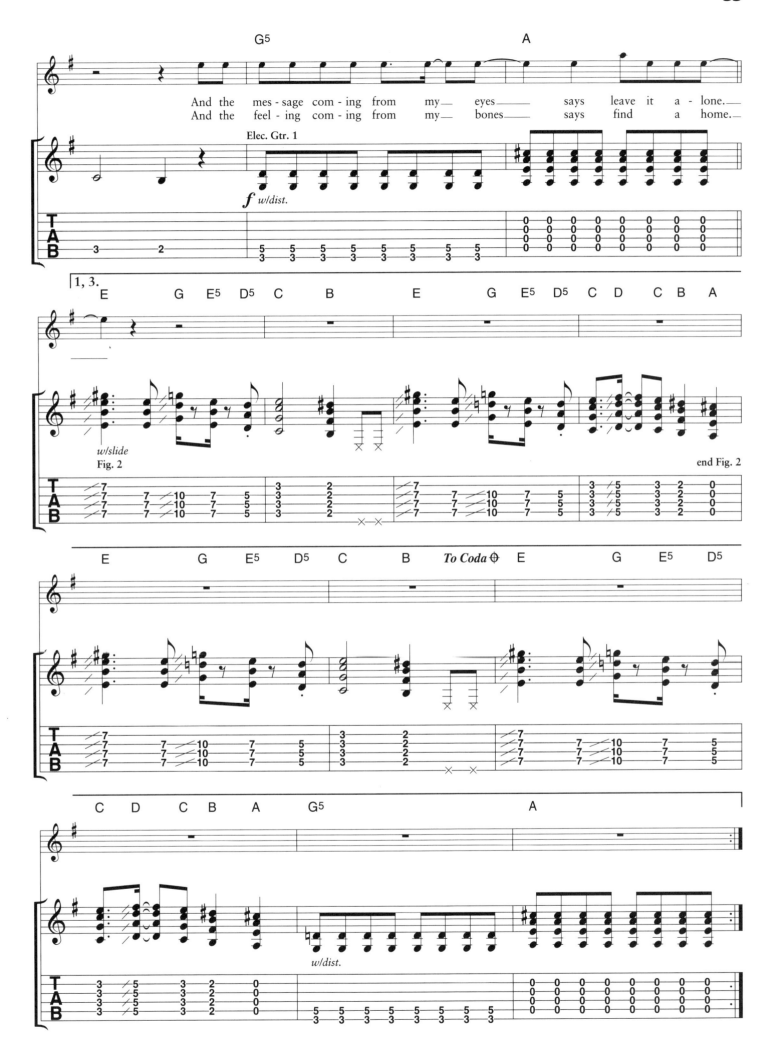

And the mes-sage com-ing from my eyes_____ says leave it a - lone.
And the feel-ing com-ing from my bones_____ says find a home.

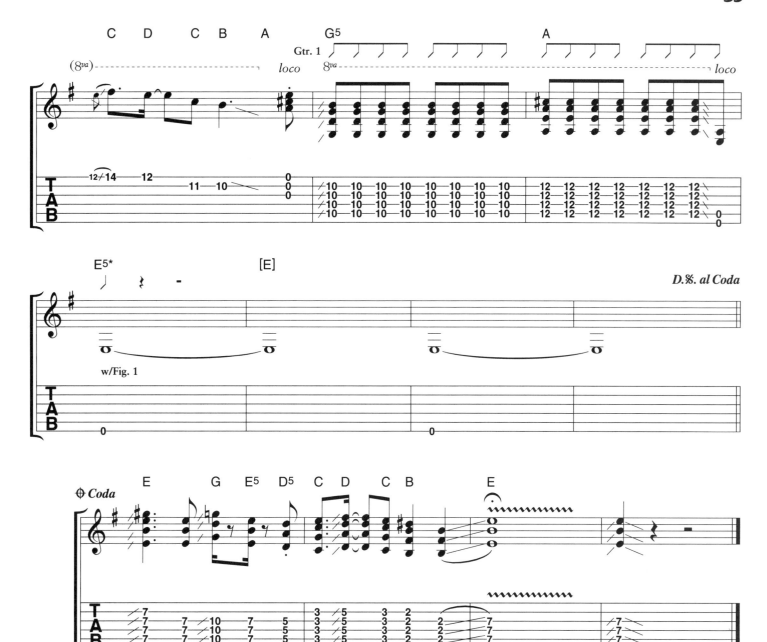

Verse 3:
I'm goin' to Wichita
Far from this opera for ever more
I'm gonna work the straw
Make the sweat drip out of every pore
And I'm bleedin' and I'm bleedin'
And I'm bleedin' right before the Lord
All the words are gonna bleed from me
And I will think no more
And the stains coming from my blood
Tells me go back home.

Silence Is Easy

Words and Music by James Walsh, James Stelfox, Barry Westhead and Benjamin Byrne

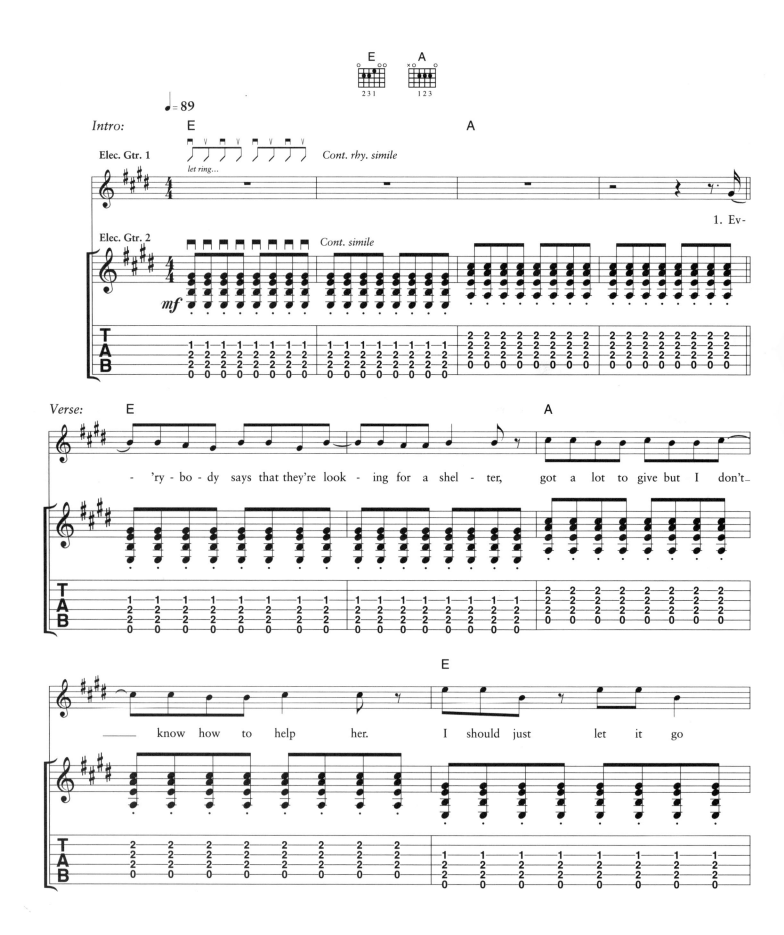

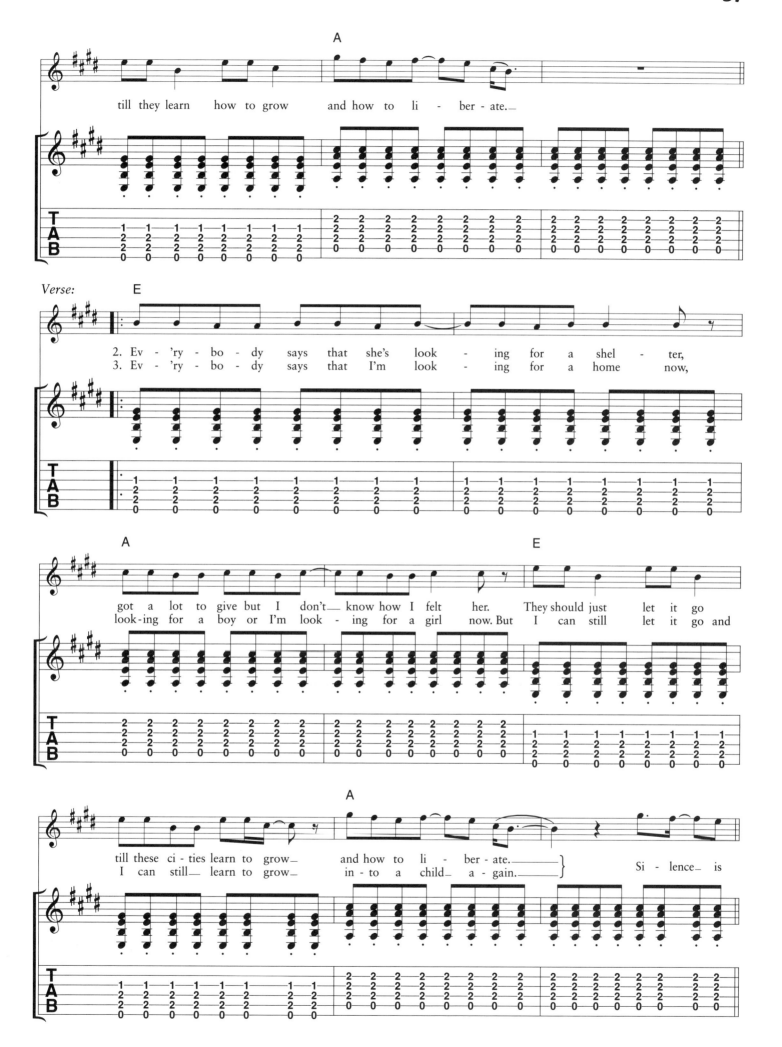

38

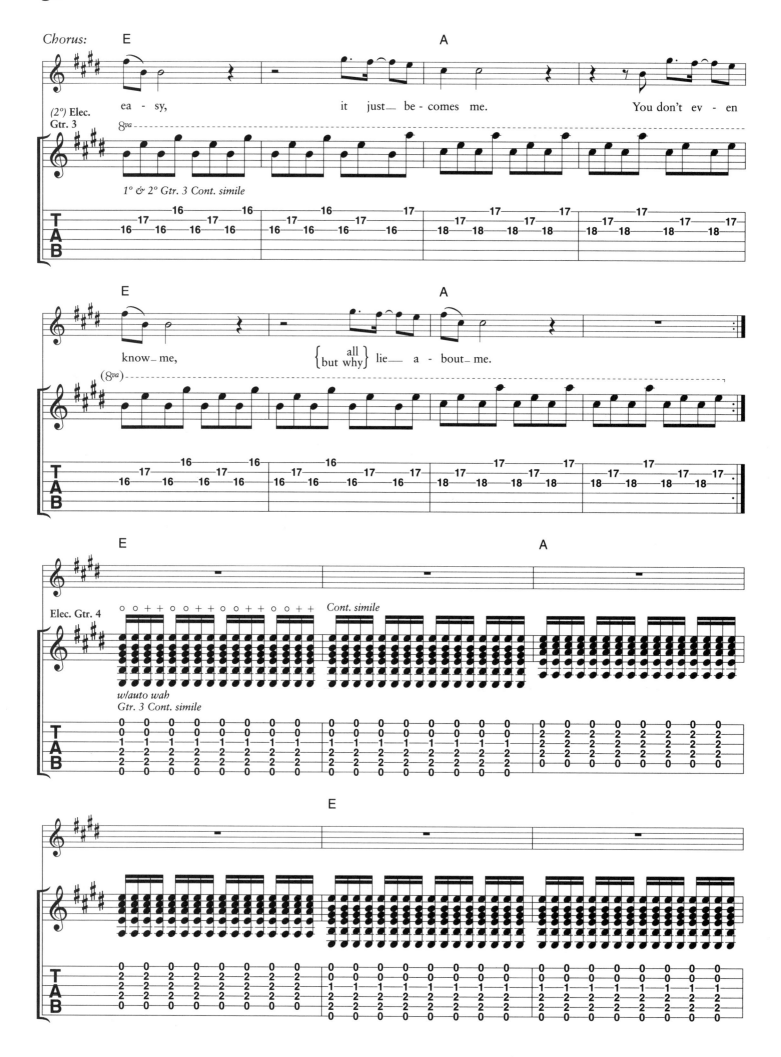

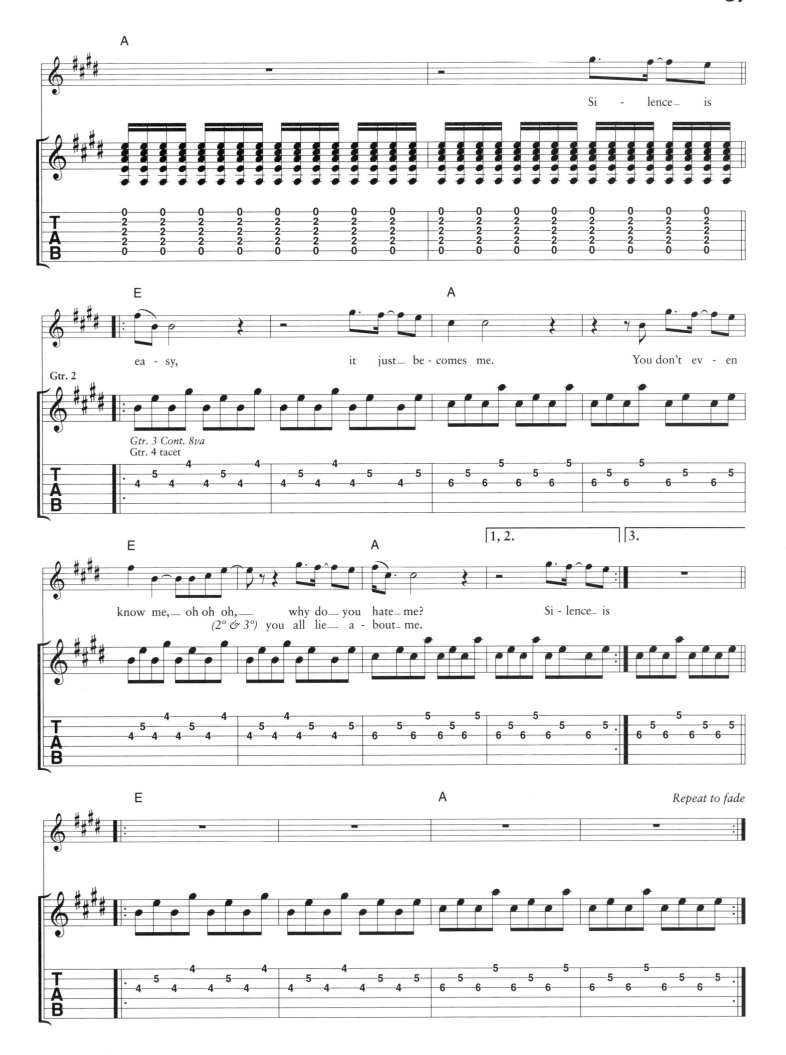

Times Like These

Words and Music by David Grohl, Taylor Hawkins, Nate Mendel and Chris Shiflett

*Chord symbols reflect combined harmony.

*Gtrs. 1, 2 & 3: w/ Rhy. Fig. 1 (2 times)

*w/ dist.

Verse

1. I,   I'm a one___ way mo - tor - way,
2. I,   I'm a new___ day ris - ing,

* let ring throughout

*Next 6 meas.

B   C5   E5

End Rhy. Fig. 4

I'm a road ___ that drives ___ a - way ___ and fol - lows you ___ back home. ___
I'm a brand ___ new sky ___ to hang ___ the stars ___ up - on ___ to - night. ___

End Riff C

Gtrs. 1, 2 & 3: w/ Rhy. Fig. 1

Gtr. 1: w/ Riff C
Gtr. 2: w/ Rhy. Fig. 4

D7add6   *D

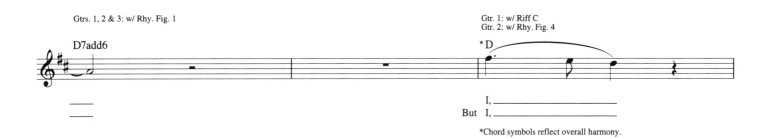

___   I, _____
___   But I, _____

*Chord symbols reflect overall harmony.

Am7

I'm a street - light shin - ing,   I'm a white ___ light blind -
I'm a lit - tle di - vid - ed.   Do I stay ___ or run ___

**Gtrs. 1, 2 & 3: w/ Rhy. Fig. 1 (2 times)

C   Em7   D7add6

- ing bright, ___ burn - ing off ___ and on. ___
___ a - way ___ and leave ___ it all ___ be - hind? ___

**w/ dist.

Uh. _____
Uh. _____   It's times ___

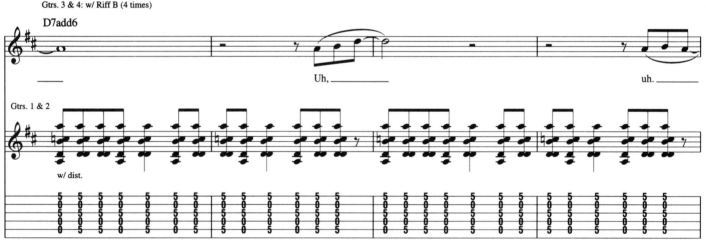

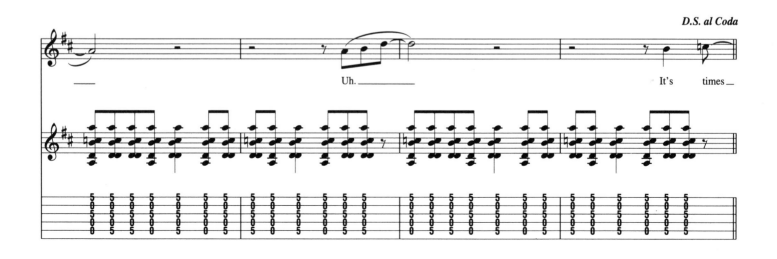

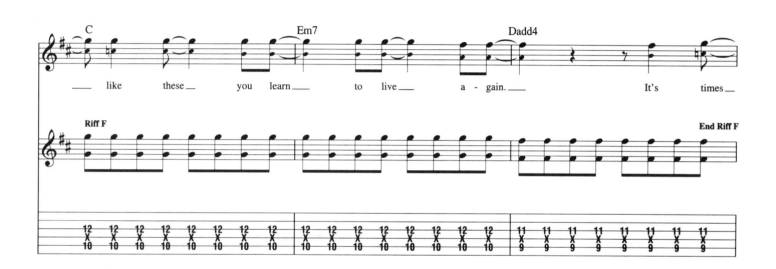

Outro